**Soma Ito**

 **@ SomaPoetry**

 **Soma_Ito_Poetry**

 **SomaIto.Bogspot.com**

SOMA ITO

MY DEAREST

First Published in December 2015.
Published by Amos H.W.M.

All rights reserved. No Part of this publication may be reproduced or transmitted in any form or by means electronic or mechanical, including photocopying, recording or any information storage or retrieval system without the prior permission from
Amos H.W.M.

This book is a work of fiction. Names, characters, places and incidents either are the product of the author's imagination or are used fictitiously. Any resemblance to actual persons, living or dead, events or locales is entirely coincidental.

ISBN 9789810976729

Cover Concept by Amos H.W.M.
Cover Design by Ikira
Cover Illustration by Ikira

Email: soma_ito@hotmail.com

About Author

This is the first book written by Author Soma Ito. His gradual works and his latest one will show you his growing sincere feelings for the mistress of his works.

You will understand the author's life and reason of writing through his works.

He hid in his shadow after losing his first love, he lost his spirit for years without knowing it was actually lost. He walked through 4 years of his life in a shell with no soul. To understand, the sincere romance of his work.

Read on… Understand our author's love for his precious heroine, which sound familiar to anyone who was in love before.

~Editor's Note

Copyright © 2015 Soma Ito

All rights reserved.

ISBN: 9789810976729
ISBN-13: 9789810976729

'The girl I once loved left silently with the angels.'

My Dearest

'My Dearest', an important word to give you a status in my heart,

Two words combine under a process known as suffocating love.

Two young lovers never want to separate till after death,

One left leaving him alone on earth,
Still she conquered his playful heart and gave him weapons he never need.

She, an angel who came to his dream, her soul talks to him when he is depressed.

She, a girl with sharp tongue became warm and loving after her farewell.

He needs no girl just her.

He is indubitably having their forbidden love, where no humans can see with their naked eye.

Only with his naked heart to feel his love for her.

I will wait, keep waiting and wait.

I will find you soon someday.

Leaving this cell and search for you.

Life is an eternal prison without you 'My Dearest', my love for you till eternity.'

~Soma

Roam with Regret

'When my memories did sank deep down into the deepest oceans of my heart.

I hope these memories will change and light up my world.

I will stay in this place eternally, waiting for you to light back my world.

The rain laughs at my memories with tears, the thunder tremble my heart and filled me with courage.

I look forward to face the pain and regret in the past with many deep scars, as that was not attended in my heart for a long time.

The nature did their best to support me by transforming those pain and regret in my life into strength, so to walk toward a new path but is not easy without you, now I am stuck in this world alone with regrets of my past.'

Your love still exist

'I see your smile, behind the clouds

I see your blush, behind the moon

I see your worried face, behind the stars

I feel your presence, behind the sun.

Your love still exist.'

~Soma

Little hope

'I hope the world can be shrunk with my love.

I hope the people along the way will guide me to you.

To let me hold your hands once again.'

~Soma

Was it my Fantasy?

'Most memories of you have vanished slowly.

I wonder was these memories fantasy.

All that has left was your soft smile, which appears when I close my eyes, thinking of you.

The words you encourage me when I am depressed.'

~Soma

Pageant

'Our love have yet became pageant.

Our history has long stopped when the day you left.

I wish the day our new history begins will be a pageant to our kids.'

~Soma

Color Blind

'Colors of the sunflower.

Colors of the roses.

I was unable to see the beauty in them again.

You had their rights with you.

When heaven took you away, the sudden farewell.

My life became a pallid world.'

~Soma

Promises

You never fail to fulfill the promises that we had made.

These are the promises; I failed...

Never to forget our memories...
Not to cry anymore;
Never look at other girl, as you are perfect for me.

I forgot about you, after your sudden farewell.
I erased memories of us and the promises that will never come to light again.
The promises came to haunt me along with the precious memories of us.

My tears never ending.'

~Soma

Unattached

My ego

My pride

My personality

I prefer to suffer the sufferings alone.

You are my worries, the girl who I missed for years.

I chose to remain unattached.

I believe our hearts are still connected.'

~Soma

Nobody

'Nothing would change even how much I shout.

Nobody will show me the path to you.

Even how much I beg heaven to answer my prayer...

Memories are evidence, you left me.'

~Soma

Pages

'The pages written with memories of us as reference.

The poems, I wrote for you.

I wish you could feel my despair hidden between every line from each poem.'

~Soma

Pray tonight, message to you

'How far are we away from heaven?

I ask myself as I watch astronauts go to the moon.

Heaven seems like a word which sound close but reality we are far away from it.

You went there alone without any farewell.

You went there before I heard your last words.

Now, all I can do is to pray and wish the moon and stars will send my blessing to you.'

~Soma

Missing you, under the lonely sky

'I start to sleep in the garden for a simple reason.

I wish I could still feel your presence in the night.

I wish when I am awake the next day, you will hug me.

I wish I would have a dream of you.

I wish the nature would lead your soul to me.

I pray to the night sky before I sleep.

I stretch my hand as I look up to the starry night.

I wish I can reach out to you because I really miss you.'

~**Soma**

My dream, Your appearance

'Sometimes, I fell asleep during the day.

The short nap became a long one.

You came into my dream; we talk and talk but is like a system you made.

I kept forgot to say the three special words.

Whenever I walk alone, I feel your presence and warmth wrapping around my arm.'

~Soma

Antidote

'My first happiness, I am losing the will to retrieve it back.

All I need now is an antidote for a loss of words to describe our past.'

~Soma

Like Seasons

Both of us are like Autumn,

Both of us appear as heaven calls upon us.

Yet we vanish when the Winter comes;

As the piles of snow covered our love and memories.

~Soma

Numb my heart, for you

'I bury myself under the Avalanche.

With a hope to numb my love for you.

I closed my eyes hard searching for you.

I cried as the last smile was bury deep in me.

I hope my feelings remain deep for you as the river continues to flow.'

~**Soma**

Daily battle

'I listen to the rain with my eyes shut.

I battle the sun with my eyes wide.

I watch the azure clouds as it collides.

For a reason to search for you.'

~Soma

Desperate, on a hunt for you

'I want to know where you are,

This desperate feeling made my heart burnt.

This time I will be the one to lock you.

I kept describing you to my parents,

They do not bother about you,

Soon I wonder did our love exist in this world.'

~Soma

Forgive me

You are a committed girl,

You never failed to bring me back to the right path,

I know you will be frustrated at me if you see me today.

I became a total different person from that day.

All these which you wanted me to avoid, I became most of them…forgive me.

~Soma

My Rose

'You broke my ego and principle for a purpose.

You create a new ego and principles for me.

You want me to be a better man for myself.

You scolded me for giving in to my anger.

You slap me for being childish.

You calm down and hug me.

You apologize despite it was my fault.

You cried instead of me.

You walk to heaven yourself with a hope.

A hope to make me a better man despite the distance.'

~**Soma**

Dream

'I woke up in my timeless room.
I can hear the sound of rain.
The morning light became dark and lonely.
I went back to sleep with a wish to meet you.
A moment where I can calm you during the storm.'

~Soma

Raindrops

'Raindrops on the window.
I cannot explain my feelings as I look.
It feels nostalgic like a short movie of us.
You once told me the raindrops on the window;
It represent the tears of love being change;
I laugh and call it weird.
The day you left, I watch the raindrops land on my window.
To me, the raindrops on my window;
It feels that tears of lover being separated with loneliness as it sticks to my window with a hope for warmth.'

~Soma

Clown

I hide my despair behind a mask.
A mask filled with many characters.
Showing my comedian and fierce emotions.
A barrier to hide my despair missing you.
I hide my sadness behind the mask.
I do not need pity from people.
I do not need people to know you.
I do not need to search for you.
I believe we will meet if fate help us once more.
I soon forget about my tears and emotions.
I mess up my life with no honesty on my feeling.
I tried to cry but it became impossible.
The hard breathing to force a cry as I miss you.
I am a clown today for others.'

Eye

Flashback of our last moment.

Your pair of watery eyes tried to tell me something.

Your pair of eyes reflect a tingle of loneliness.

Your tears were the signal to our last farewell.

I was a fool back then, if I knew these were the hints of your departure.

~Soma

Nature

I just learn to admire the sound of nature,

I just realize the beauty of my inner peace.

I just escaped reality-

Nature became my remedy to heal my broken heart.

'I am sorry' The three words from your mouth-

Traumatized my innocent eye when I tried to sleep and choked my mind.

                              ~**Soma**

Wither

'Ever since that day of your sudden departure-

I have been living life as per normal. Ever since the day of memories haunt me-

I have been living life like a withered cherry blossom that will never bloom its happiness again.'

~Soma

Lost Memories Under Time

'If back then, I knew nothing last forever.

If, I knew time would never fail to drain one soul...

I would have be more honest with myself,

I would have treated you, the way you treated me.

I miss the way you cling to me every moment.

If, I can no longer reach out for our dream-
I will just bury myself in our past till old.

~Soma

An Unrequited love

We wish for a love that will be simple.

We pray for a love that will be blissful and without pain.

After many wishes and hopes, we realize our delusion are just our fantasy in reality

Our one-sided hope and wish, is an evidence of our unrequited love.

~Soma

Our Usual Route

'I walk the lonely dark street with only the moon as my light and the stars as my courage.

As I walk down the dark lonely street, I hope to see you at the end of the street.

Indeed when I reach the end of the street, I smile with tears, knowing that you are far beyond the end of street or earth, even universe.

You are in a faraway paradise.'

~**Soma**

Feelings

'I wrote my days on my diary each night.
I have no place to discard my feelings for you-
The diary is my only place to connect both hearts as one again.
Even after you have long gone to paradise, I am still a coward who still cannot express my words honestly.
The feelings you gave me with genuine love and wholeheartedly is on the verge of vanquished-
Memories of you returned now, before my feelings for you defeated by my daily life.
I will not accept the fact you left with the angels, I will embrace the 'impossibility' for us to meet once again.'

~ **Soma**

Only You

'You are the one and only you, nobody can replace.

You are unique, unlike most girls-

The reason for me to hold you still is my childish feeling.

I will connect the stars with my imagination, to create a visual image of you and have a long night chat.

I cherish you and will love you as long as my heart still wish for you, even knowing you are above beyond our reach.'

~Soma

Star

'If your sudden departure was not fate, if you are still somewhere around this world-

If you are upset about your existence, I will let you be my only star again and shine upon our love.

True happiness is when both of us are together, even if there are situation when we will argue-

You are still the only one star to remain in my heart.'

                                              ~Soma

Be With You

'I want to see you, if there's not a single reason for you to live on beneath the boundless clear sky-

Just a word from you, I will run to you even if the field of magnetism go against me.

I will admire every emotions display through your eyes, pain or happiness;

I want to be with you.'

~Soma

Look

My look, my build, my personality, my eyes-

People are scared of it, my 'gorilla-sized' became a viral name for me.

My 'cool' personality, none of them knew I prefer silence.

My eyes, a pair of eyes filled with frustration...
I am like a wild gorilla, surviving the harshness of reality-

Hoping for you to tear this despair world for me and show me a new world like back then.'

~**Soma**

Faith

I yet to understand word faith,

My emotions run wildly like spirits around me.

I search frantically for you deep down my soul.

I just want to find that last smile and keep it.

I lost it as time pass without a warning.'

~Soma

Wish

'The words, I wished to tell you became regret.

The chances I had was blown away by destiny.

I wish somewhere soon, as you read my works.

You will uncover the messages I wanted you to hear between the lines.

The million tears I shed in each poetry.

Your last smile, your existence were the reason of my million tears and poems.'

~**Soma**

Diary

'I write a personal diary to talk with you.

I know it is impossible for you to read.

I need a comfort for myself to say you are alive.

It feels like a friend of a coma patient.

Friends talk to the coma patient with no reply.

I write my diary with 'Hey' and 'I remember once'.

It really consoles me that you are beside me.

I wrote a serious diary about my regret and grief then head to sleep.

You appear in my dream, talk to me with a smile, and hug to console me.

The temporary warmth after so long caused me to cry like an infant as I woke up.'

~Soma

Rescue

' I loved and still love you for not your looks nor personality

You noticed me when I despised both my existence and the world.

You rescued me from my dark world and shower me with thin droplets of love.

~Soma

'Want' to Conquer

'I want to conquer the sky and free you.

I want to conquer the memories of us.

I want to conquer the love you gave.

I want to conquer my grey emotionless world.'

~Soma

First time

'Every human have a first time.

Our first time brought excitement after accomplishing it.

I had done many first times in life but it was not on my own will.

You kiss me the first time, hug me the first time and make me blush for the first time.

These are your wills and it made me glad you were the first to take my first time.

You may be faraway for time being, these memories when I shut my eyes close still tremble my heart with excitement.'

~Soma

Direction

You were my direction;

Heading towards the crimson;

Looking back and forth for a sign to lead me.

I lost my direction under the 'light' without you.

~Soma

Opposite ends

'I feel the distance in us.

It feels unreal.

An Axis that rotate our world differently.'

~Soma

Separation

'With the breeze passing me.

Time froze at my pace.

Angels pity my despair heart.

Angels brought you to my life to save me.

Devil jealous our love and broke us apart.

~Soma

Stuck without you

'I lock myself in my wide room with darkness.

I cannot see the day and night.

I dare not see the time and month.

I lie on the bed looking at the ceiling.

I felt hopeless without you.

I found a goal with you.

I lost the will to reach the goal without you.

I walk on the clock in my imaginary world.

I felt our memories became eternal when I shut my eyes.'

~Soma

Why am I crying?

'Why do we have tears?

Why do I cry when I am strong?

Why do I hear your warm encouraging words, when I am about to give up?'

~Soma

Save it for you

'Humid air during the rain felt like a dark stuffy cell.

It is the same as I am trying to find you,

Holding back all my words I want to say,

Just to let you be the first to hear.

It feels like an asthma with no relieve.'

~Soma

Once our fun, now a depressing rain

'I listen to a sad song during rainy days.

I do not want to experience the sound of rain without you.

I do not need the heaven's pity for they are the one who took you away from me.'

~Soma

You were my eyes

'Walking beside you, the things I never notice became important to me.

Pots of flower along the roadside, trees and birds chirping.

I notice all of these living things beside you.

You held my hand, as you were afraid I got lost in the crowd.

My heart palpitated because I am afraid of losing you.

Despite our promise, our lives are still under heaven's watch.

You went ahead of me with the angels.'

~Soma

Suffocate

'The conversation we once had.

The promises we once wrote on our palm.

The tears we shed before you depart from this world.

I suffocate as memories choke me.'

~Soma

Blind

When you are around, I never knew how valuable you worth until fate took you away, which is beyond my reach.

I can only regret and wait for miracle, because I know nobody knows me and love me as much as you did.'

~Soma

My first warmth

'You were like a cop back then chasing after me till the end of earth.

You caught me with a handcuff and a promise never to let me go.

I tried to hold back my tears because you gave my first warmth.

Your warmth and hug was like a spell as it release my tears uncontrollably.'

~Soma

Realization

My mind start to daydream, as I stare in daze.

Memories flashback, I realize my life once have someone who is genuine and care for me back then.

I treated her as dust, now she is a treasure which I cannot reach out to.'

~Soma

Time

'Time is a traumatizing monster, is time a poison or an antidote?

All I know, time silently wash away my happiest memories.'

~Soma

City in the sky

'A city in the sky, I justified the fact of its existence still deep down in my heart.

I wish it does exist because the day I depart from earth, I hope we can start anew there.

Time devour my heart alive, before I could meet you once again.'

~**Soma**

Evade

'I want to feel the numbness in my arms;

I want to escape reality once again, just a little.

Losing you, was my worst failure in life

Because, you could never return to earth nor my arms anymore.'

~Soma

Hey, my worries

'Hey, are you eating well?

Hey, are you cold?

Hey, do you miss me as much as I do?

Hey, let's close our eyes and close the gap within us.'

~Soma

Small steps

'You walk out of my world like a defeated general, without a word said.

Your small steps towards my life brought no harm but warmth and love

Yet, your small steps out of my life brought a pain that cannot be cure.

I will search on for a place where time will rotate back to the past, awaiting for you.'

~Soma

Meaningless

'Will a poetry and song be meaningless, if the person I wrote for unable to read it?

What is meaningless?

Never…in my heart and mind, your soul is always with me.

I know I can only put in words to tell you that our love is true;

our love is precious;

Our love is never-ending.'

~Soma

Truth

'I act as nothing happen, but I really miss you,

I miss you so much until I lied to myself that you are alive.

Truth and facts cannot be change in history that you left with the Angels.'

~Soma

Lonely

'My heart is trapped within me.

The buildings around me and the impregnable sky trapped my body.

I am lonely without you;

The only communication between us is my pen and diary.'

~Soma

Reason

'I just need a reason of your sudden departure.

I just need a reason to end my everlasting faithfulness.

I just need a reason from the angels, the reason they took you away.

I just need a reason for my 'lost' autumn, which will never return from the pile of snow.

Was my love for you buried under the snow, the reason for my everlasting faithfulness?'

~Soma

You

'The moments with you will never come again.

The moment of my unstable excited heartbeat-

I will never experience it anymore.

Having memories of you returned to me once again-

It is enough to let you know my heart still belongs to you.'

~Soma

Quotes

'Time devour my heart alive, before I could meet you once again.'
~Soma

'The heavy downpour blind the beauty before me, like millions of events in my life vanquishing my past memories of us.'
~Soma

'I am willing to wait for you till night, as long as it take for us to meet once again-
When both angels and devils will never interfere us.'
~Soma

'It is painful to say goodbye, knowing it will be eternally.
It is painful to say goodbye, understanding that there will not be any chance.
It is painful not saying goodbye and realize she is no longer here with me. '

Quotes

'With the breeze passing me.
Time froze at my pace.
Angel pity my despair heart.
Angel brought you to my life to save me.
Devil envy our love and broke us apart.'
～Soma

'Silence is an everlasting remedy and pain for me.
I am silent most of the time, thinking of your life in a foreign land beyond earth.
Silence is one cure to my broken heart.'
～Soma

'You squeak excitedly like a mouse.
I chase you like a cat angrily.
You cheekily escape from my paws.
Our life became a catching game.
I am still chasing you with a hope in me.'
～Soma

'

'I believe that everyone has a quote or story they want to express deeply, to explode their emotions and let one know. I believe, some quotes are related to your life, why not write it below here and #SomaMyQuote'   ~Soma

_____

_____

_____

SOMA ITO

www.ingramcontent.com/pod-product-compliance
Lightning Source LLC
Chambersburg PA
CBHW071412040426
42444CB00009B/2214